YOUTH A

Contents

1
Who is Jesus?

Christianity is not about a 'blind faith'.

It's a faith based on FACT.

Jesus existed, there is overwhelming evidence.

"Its all true."

Fact one: It's not just the Bible that talks about Jesus. Jewish and Roman historians said...
"There was at that time Jesus, a wise man, if indeed we should call him a man!"

Fact two: Another guy reported... "Christ suffered the extreme penalty during the reign of Tiberius at the hands of Pontius Pilate."

Fact three: He had real feelings and emotions just like you and me. He really did and said amazing things.

* He had a body that got tired and hungry.
  Check out: John 4:6, Matthew 4:2

* He had emotions of anger, love and sadness.
  check out Mark 11:15-17, Mark 10:21, John 11:32-36

* He experienced life! Learning, working, obeying etc
  Check out: Luke 2:46-52, Mark 6:3, Luke 2:51, Mark 1:13

He really existed! But surely he was only a good teacher? Jesus said a lot about himself and what he'd come for.

He said he could...

...Satisfy our spiritual needs   John 6:35
...Show us the way to God   John 14:6
...Bring light into our lives   John 8:12

1. What did he say about himself?

He was...God   John 14:9
He could...forgive sins   Mark 2:5
He would...judge the world   Matthew 25:31-32

Would you ask people to...
... "Come to me"   Matthew 11:28-29
... "Follow me"   Mark 1:17
... "Receive me"   Matthew 10:40

Jesus did say those things and his friends called him...

"My Lord and my God." John 20:28

"A man who was just a man and said the sort of things that Jesus said wouldn't be a great moral teacher, he'd either be a lunatic - on a level with a man who says he's a poached egg - or else he'd be the devil of hell. You must make your choice...!"   C.S.Lewis

2. How did Jesus back up what he'd said?

* His teaching was practical   Matthew 5,6,7
* He did amazing things   John 11:43
* His own character
* He fulfilled Old Testament promises
* He beat death

3. How do you know that he came back from the dead?

No sign of him in the tomb.
    EXPLANATION?

    - He didn't die!
    - His friends stole his body!
    - Romans stole it!

"...um, we thought you might be interested in this you guys."

BUT, **Check out:** John 20:1-10.
His clothes were untouched.

    - He did die. John 19:34 a medical sign of death.
    - What use would a dead body be to his friends?
    - If the Romans had stolen his body, surely they
      would have dragged it out when the disciples
      said "he's alive".

* He appeared to lots of people.
   EXPLANATION?
   -Hallucination or a Ghost.

BUT,

> **Fact:** 550+ people saw Jesus on 11 different occasions over a six week period.

* Immediate effect on people. The church grew so fast.

* People experience the same Jesus today.

Wrapping it up...!

Who do you say Jesus is then?

Madman... Thought he was God, but wasn't.

Badman... Knew he wasn't God, out to con people.

God-man... God come to us as a man.

The choice is yours!

2
Why did Jesus die?

How many people do you know who wear a cross?
Ever seen someone wear a......... little electric chair?

> "The cross was one of the cruellest
> forms of execution known to man."

So why is the cross shown as the symbol of the Christian
faith?

> The cross....is the answer to the
> PROBLEM!

1. So, what's the problem ?

It's the rubbish that clutters up our
lives, and clutters our world.

This rubbish pollutes all of us!

Fact: The Bible has a word
for this rubbish... Sin!
Sin is pollution of the soul!

Check out: Mark 7:21-23

Fact: Any legal fine
has to be paid!

More than that. This rubbish cuts us off from a
friendship with God. It gets in the way, leaving
us feeling dead on the inside. Often guilty.

BUT

God doesn't want us to stay guilty. He loves us too
much for that. He wants to forgive. Give us a
fresh start!

2. <u>What could God do about the problem?</u>

1) IGNORE IT   2) FORGET IT   3) SORT IT

Check out: 1 Peter 2:24

God didn't ignore it or forget it but he came as Jesus
To SORT IT! Take a second to think what Jesus went
through on the cross...for you.

3. <u>How did the cross deal with the sin problem?</u>

Check out: Romans 3:23

God didn't want us to get the death sentence for our
sin . So, Jesus stood in our place. He died instead of
us.

He took the rubbish off us and onto himself. That means we can be free of the rubbish that keeps us guilty and ruins our friendship with God.

Wrapping it up...!

In his death, Jesus removed the blockage of sin. He rescued us from its power and brought us face to face ith God again. Because Jesus beat DEATH, he's shown us that he's beaten sin as well.

It's only Jesus who ever did this!

Check out: Galatians 2:20

3
How can I be sure of my faith?

Fact: God wants us to be sure of our friendship with him.

Check out: 1 John 5:13

Here are three solid things that help us to be sure of our friendship with God.

1. What God promises.

REMEMBER that Christianity doesn't just rely on feelings, which can change! But on the power of Jesus who is reliable and never changes.

Check out: These promises that Jesus makes.

"I will come in" to your life when you ask!
Revelation 3:20

"I am with you always"
Matthew 28:20

"I give them eternal life...no-one can snatch them out of my Father's hand" John 10:28-29

| **Faith is** sticking on a blindfold, leaving your brain at the door and leaping into the blackness hopefully! | **Faith is** taking the things that God has said and daring to believe them! |

2. What God has done.

You can't earn God's forgiveness. Nobody's <u>that</u> good. Jesus died on the cross to bring us back to God.

GOD   MAN

* Jesus loves us and died to prove it!
   Check out: John 3:16
* He took our sins on himself.
   Check out: Isaiah 53:6, 1 Peter 2:24

3. What God keeps doing!

When someone becomes a Christian, God's Holy Spirit comes to live in them.

* He changes us from the inside out.

i) Our characters become more like Jesus.
   Check out: Galatians 5:22

ii) Our friendship with others.

Question: what changes have there been aready in your life?

- More interest in God?
- Feel different?
- Read the Bible?
- Want to help other people?
- Desire to worship?

---

* He makes me realise, deep inside, that I'm his child.

Check out: Romans 8:15-16

4
Why and How should I read the Bible?

You can't say you don't believe it, until you've taken time to read it.

"i've never read it. — but its stupid — I know"

> **Fact:** 44 million Bibles are sold each year. It's <u>the</u> best-seller of all time.

Question: So, what's in it then?

* Lots of books and stories in one cover.
  66 books, 40 different authors, written over 1500 years.

* Full of real people's stories and their problems...
  fear, jealousy, hatred, murder, sex scandals,
  violence...it's all there!

Question: How do I know it's not all made up?

A lot of the Bible is history, and matches up with other historical writings. But the Bible also includes poetry, wisdom, laws, letters, songs and prophecy (messages from God). The evidence for the accuracy of the New Testament is more impressive than the evidence for Caesar's Gallic Wars. No historian doubts the truth of that.

Check out: Matthew 4:4

The Bible is powerful. It offers us the opportunity to meet with the living God. If God is alive, then surely he wants to talk to his people. One of the ways he does that is through the Bible.

1. <u>God Speaks - the manual for life.</u>

Christianity is not about us trying to get to God. It's God showing himself to us. God showed himself to us as Jesus. God keeps showing himself through the pages of the Bible. It's a living book and not dead history!

Check out: 2 Timothy 3:16
"All scripture is God-breathed and is useful for..."

The Bible is 100% the work of people. It's also 100% inspired by God. He's breathed life into it! He did this so that as we read these "living words" , we can find out what to believe and how to live.

The Bible is not just about rules, although rules can be a good thing. Imagine a game of football with no rules. Rules bring order.

2. God speaks about a relationship.

Check out: John 5:39-40

The main point of the Bible is to show us how to be in a relationship with God through Jesus.

Check out: 2 Timothy 3:15

It's often as people read the New Testament that they put their trust in Jesus. Even people who've been Christians for years say how God still speaks through the Bible.

Reading it helps us...

* Become like Jesus
* Have joy and peace
* Receive guidance
* Receive healing
* Be protected
* Come under God's power
* Get cleaned up!

2 Corinthians 3:18
Psalm 23:5
Psalm 119:105
Proverbs 4:20-22
Matthew 4:1-11
Hebrews 4:12
John 15:3

3. How can I hear God speak through the Bible?

a) **Take time** to read a bit each day.
b) **Plan** when and where you'll do it.
c) **Get help**! (use Bible reading notes)
d) **Ask God** to speak to you as you read.
e) **Ask yourself...**
   What does the passage say? What does it mean?
   How does it apply to my life?
f) **Talk to God** about it.
g) **Put what you read into practice**...DO IT!

Wrapping it up...!

Keep growing, Keep going and keep glowing!
Psalm 1:1-3

5
Why and How do I Pray?

"Hands together, head bowed, eyes closed...**Z Z Z Z** zz !"

FACT: Three quarters of the population of this country admit to praying at least once a week.

---

1. <u>So, what is prayer then?</u>

* Do you pray when life gets tough or things go wrong?
* Do you pray when things are going well?
* How would you feel if your best friend only contacted you when they were in trouble?

God wants a day by day friendship with us, through the good and the bad of life!

Check out: Matthew 6:5-13
                 Ephesians 2:18
                 Romans 8:26

We pray...   a) To our Father in heaven.
                 b) In Jesus' name.
                 c) Helped by the Holy Spirit.

2. <u>Why pray?</u>

Because it's the main way we develop our friendship with God. What could be more important than that?
Jesus spent hours praying.

hello.

Check out: Mark 1:35

He told his followers to do the same.
DID YOU KNOW...

3. <u>God always answers prayer.</u>

We're very quick to ask, but what about waiting for the answer? God may answer our prayers by saying "YES", "NO" or "WAIT".

Dear Lord.....
um, maybe a porshe

He might even tell us that we're praying for the wrong thing.

Sometimes our attitudes may stop God from answering our prayers.

    a) Not forgiving someone.
    b) Disobeying God.
    c) Asking for wrong things.
    d) Hidden sin.

4. <u>OK, how should we pray then?</u>

A good place to start is the Lord's Prayer that we looked at earlier. You can pray that a line at a time. Pause between each line to add in your own prayers. ie "Hallowed be your name", "Lord, I'll live my life in worship of you".

Fact: People finish prayers by saying, "In Jesus' name" or "Through Jesus Christ our Lord", because it's through Jesus that we have access to God.

Some people use this method... **T.S.P.**

Thanks Thanking God for who he is, for his love, for Jesus. Thanks for family/friends etc.

Sorry Saying sorry for the things we've done/ thought/said wrong. Asking God to forgive us.

Please Praying for ourselves, our friends and for others in the world.

5. When should we pray?

It's good to pray throughout the day whatever you're doing.

Check out: 1 Thessalonians 5:17, Ephesians 6:18

It's good to fix a time each day to pray alone.

Check out: Matthew 6:6

Some people find it best to pray in the morning, others at night. Find what's best for your lifestyle.

It's also important to pray with others.

Check out: Matthew 18:19

" Thanks Father ... amen "

This can be embarrassing at first.
Once you're used to it though it
builds your faith up...
...and your friendships too!

6
Who is the Holy Spirit?

The Holy Spirit is <u>not</u>

a Ghost or a Ghoul!

He is the third part of God. God is Father, Son and Holy Spirit.

 FATHER SON  HOLY SPIRIT

God's Holy Spirit comes to live in us when we become Christians.

The Holy Spirit is therefore a "HE" and not an "IT".
So, we can't ignore him and mustn't resist him.

1. In the Old Testament.

* He was involved in creating the world...
Check out: Genesis 1:2

...and people too
Check out: Genesis 2:7

* He came upon some people to help them do special jobs for God.

- An artist called Bezalel. Exodus 31:1-5
- A leader named Gideon. Judges 6:14-16,34
- A warrior called Samson. Judges 15:14-15
- A prophet named Isaiah. Isaiah 61:1-3

* A new thing was promised!

- Lots of people will know God. Jeremiah 31:31-34
- The Holy Spirit not 'ON' but 'IN' people.
  Ezekiel 36:26-27
- No-one is to be left out. Joel 2:28

These promises took 300 years to come about.
Jesus made these promises come true!

2. In the New Testament.

a) At the time of Jesus' birth the Holy
   Spirit was busy with these people!

   - John the Baptist. Luke 1:15
   - Jesus' mother Mary. Luke 1:35
   - Elizabeth. Luke 1:41

   But still the Holy Spirit was only with a few people.

b) John the Baptist tells us what Jesus was going to do.

Check out: Luke 3:16

The Holy Spirit poured into us.
Filling the empty bits of our
lives with the Spirit.

c) Jesus was a man filled with the Holy Spirit.

   Check out: Luke 4:1, 14, 18

d) Jesus promised that the Holy Spirit would be received.

   Check out: John 7:37-39

e) He tells his disciples to wait in the city
   for the Spirit to come... and he did.

   Check out: Acts 2:4-12

   The disciples received...new languages...
   new boldness...new power!

Wrapping it up...!

We now live in the age of the Holy Spirit. God's promise of sending his Spirit has happened. It's a promise for you and me. God has promised to give his Spirit to every Christian.

Check out: Acts 2:38-39

7
What does the Holy Spirit do?

You were once born as a baby, right? A physical birth.

We also need to come alive on the inside too.
That means a spiritual birth. This is what happens when
we become Christians. The Holy Spirit helps us get born
again spiritually. We are born into a Christian family.

Check out: John 3:5-7

1. <u>Sons and Daughters of God.</u>

    a) All the wrong things we may have said,
       thought or done get wiped away. Romans 8:1-2

    b) We become God's sons and daughters.

      Check out: Romans 8:14-16

      * Mindblowing privilege. v.14
      * We can know him as <u>the</u>
        best Father. v.15

* Deep inside we know we're
  his. v.16
* Our future is secure with him. v.17

2. Knowing God better.

Check out: Ephesians 2:18

a) The Holy Spirit helps us to pray. Romans 8:26

b) He also helps us to understand the Bible.
   Ephesians 1:17

3. The Family likeness.

> **Fact:** We become like our friends/family as we imitate
> their habits without realising it.

The more time we spend getting to know God better,
the more we will inherit His character.

It's God's Spirit who brings this about in our lives.

Check out: Galatians 5:22-23

4. Joining the team.

The same Holy Spirit is in every Christian,
wherever they may live. But we need
to work at being united together.
This means not slagging each
other off or gossiping about
other people. Keep the unity
of the Holy Spirit! Ephesians 4:3-6

".. did you hear about
Janet.."

5. God gives us the gifts of spiritual talents.

You are unique! God wants to use you in a unique
way.

God gives Christians different gifts to help us be
useful followers of Jesus.

These gifts are brought into our lives by the Holy Spirit.

Check out: 1 Corinthians 12:1-11

Notice... a) They're free!

b) They're for each Christian.

c) They're so we can
help other people.

6. A family that grows.

The Holy Spirit helps us tell others about Jesus.

Check out: Acts 1:8

He's got the power...!

Wrapping it up...!

Every Christian has the Holy Spirit in them. But not every Christian is filled with the Holy Spirit.

Check out: Ephesians 5:18

8
How can I be filled with the Holy Spirit?

1. What happens when people experience the Spirit?

Check out: a) When it first happened Acts 2:2-4

                   b) In Samaria   Acts 8:14-17

                   c) Paul in Damascus   Acts 9:17-19

                   d) More people...   Acts 19:1-6

2. What did they experience?

Check out: These people in Samaria. Acts 10:44-46

a) The Spirit came on them...and everyone knew it!

> **Quote:** "...the Holy Spirit fell...and believers... ...were amazed" Acts 10:45

* It's obvious to others when someone gets filled, one guy even wanted to buy the power.
Acts 8:16

* Great experience of God's love for us.

Check out: Romans 5:5, Ephesians 3:14-20

b) They were praising God!

Quote: "For they heard them praising God" Acts 10:46

They got excited about God! He affected their emotions.

Forget self-conscious!...get God-conscious!

c) They spoke in a new language.

> **Quote:** "For they heard them speaking in tongues."
> Acts 10:46

* What is the gift of tongues then?

- It's talking to God in a language he gives you to use.
- It's a prayer in non-English!
- It's <u>not</u> verbal diarrhoea! You are in full control.

* So what's good about it?

- You have lots more ways to praise God. You don't
  don't have to struggle to find the right words.
- It can be a great help when you have to pray under
  pressure, ie Exams, illness, worry etc
- It helps you to pray for other people.

* Is it in the Bible? Yup! **Check out:** 1 Corinthians 14

- Don't stop it. V.39
- It's available for anyone. V.5
- Paul loved it! V.18

> **WARNING**:if someone speaks in tongues out
> loud in church, then someone else must also
> receive a translation from God of what's
> being said. That way everyone can
> understand what God is telling the church.
> (See 1 Corinthians 14:13)

* How do I receive this gift of tongues?

- Ask for it! **Check out:** 1 Corinthians 14:1

- Go with the flow! Open your mouth and begin to
  speak.

- Try on your own in your
  room.

- Believe that God wants
  to give it to you.

- Keep going with it!

3. Can anything stop me being filled with the Spirit?

Check out: Luke 11:9-13

* Being overcome
  with doubt.

* Being afraid.

* Being overcome with the
  feeling, "I'm not good enough."

Wrapping it up...!

God loves to give his Holy Spirit to people!

He's good and he'll never let us down.

Remember, you don't have to be good enough, you just have to be God's!

ASK AND RECEIVE.

9
What about the occult and resisting evil?

"The occult is only a game, a bit of fun, surely there's no harm in it...?" **WRONG!**

GOD IS GOOD! All goodness comes from him.
THE DEVIL IS EVIL! All evil springs from him.

Why do Christians believe that the devil exists?

* The Bible speaks about him. 1 Peter 5:8-11

* Our own experience of being tempted.

* Common sense when you look at the world.

1. <u>So, what is the occult?</u>

The word "occult" means "hidden things". Getting involved in occult practices means taking a step into hidden things. It means going where we were never meant to be.

2. <u>Why do people get into it and can they get out?</u>

The fact is that all people have some kind of spiritual thirst. We can try to quench that thirst in many different ways, like reading horoscopes, consulting mediums/palmists or playing with ouija boards. BUT, none of these are up to the job! What's more, they're DANGEROUS.

WARNING: You cannot be spiritual without being focused towards some spiritual force.
The choice is between GOD and SATAN.

Check out: John 6:35

* God made us with an built-in need for him.
* Only Jesus can meet that need.
* Our spiritual craving should begin and end with him!
* God is concerned to help us.
* Spiritual wholeness and peace comes through a
  friendship with Jesus.

3. What are the results of occult involvement?

When you mess about in occult things, sooner or later
those things will mess about with you.

> **FACT:** The result of encounters with unwholesome
> spiritual forces are often depression, suicidal
> tendencies and compulsive behaviour.

That is why God tells people not to get dragged
into occult practices...mediums, white/black magic,
tarot, spells, channelling, ouija boards...all are trouble!

Check out: Deuteronomy 18:9-14

4. What are the devil's tactics?

His main aim is to wreck your life.

- He's a destroyer. John 10:10
- Stops people believing in Jesus. 2 Corinthians 4:4
- Makes Christians doubt. Matthew 4:3-6
- He's a tempter. Genesis 3:6
- He'll accuse us, saying..."you're not good enough".

He'll try to stop you believing in Jesus. He'll try to tempt you off the road that leads to God.

5. How can I resist evil then?

If you've been into occult stuff, you need to turn your back on it. Get rid of anything linked with that activity, ie charms, videos, books, cards etc.

Say sorry to God, ask him to clean you up and to fill you with his Holy Spirit.

The devil may be stronger than us, but he's no match for Jesus.

Check out: Colossians 1:13

Jesus lifts us out of dark things into his light.
Into freedom, forgiveness and life.

Satan was defeated on the cross.
Colossians 2:15

Christians belong to Jesus. He gives all round and
lasting protection!

Check out: Ephesians 6:10-18

v.14 knowing the truth about God.
v.14 being made clean by Jesus.
v.15 being ready to tell others
        about Jesus.
v.16 trusting God.
v.17 salvation -
        you belong to Jesus.
 v.17 the sword -
        the Bible is a powerful weapon.

6. How do we attack?

There are three unhealthy attitudes to the devil.
- Fascination with him.
- Forgetting him.
- Fear of him.

Wrapping it up...!

God is far more powerful than any evil.
We can have his strength as we...

    ...Pray. 2 Corinthians 10:4
    ...Take action. Luke 7:22

10
How does God guide us?

* He said he would. John 10:3-4
* He wants the best for us. Jeremiah 29:11, Ephesians 2:10

BUT,

* We need to ask him. Isaiah 30:1-2
* Our attitude mustn't be cocky!

Quote: "He guides the humble in what is right and teaches them his way." Psalm 25:9 (See also Luke 1:38)

---

1. God shows us how to live through the Bible.

The Bible tells us a lot about how we should live.
eg You shouldn't hear a Christian saying, "God's told me to beat up my enemy." The Bible encourages us to "love your enemies, pray for those who persecute you."

Also, as we read the Bible, it's amazing how God uses some of the verses to speak to us.

Check out: 2 Timothy 3:16

2. <u>God speaks straight to us!</u>

As we pray, God speaks.
He gives us...
 ...strong impressions.
 ...feelings about what to do.
 ...or a thought might pop into our head!

We might feel God nudging us to do something.

He also guides in unusual ways too!

- Prophecy. Acts 11:27-28
- Dreams.   Matthew 1:20
- Visions. Acts 16:10
- Angels.   Acts 12:7
- A voice you can hear. 1 Samuel 3:4-14

All the above need testing out to see if they're really from God. Talk to others, wait a bit, check it with the Bible, ask God to say it again for you!

Check out: 1 John 4:1

3. <u>God gave us a brain to use.</u>

We don't leave our brains at the
church door when
we come in.

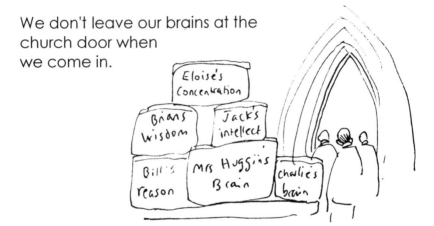

God gave us a brain so that we can think and solve
some problems ourselves!

4. <u>Other people.</u>

God can help us see things more clearly when we
talk it through with someone we trust and respect.
Whenever you think God is telling you something,
it's always good to chat it through with someone else.

5. The way events happen.

Sometimes God closes a door on us. We'd like to do something or go in a particular direction, but God says "no" by just not letting it work out!

He can also open doors of opportunity when he's saying "Yes".

Check out: 1 Corinthians 16:9

Wrapping it up...!

SO, don't rush things!

Talk issues through with someone who has more experience.

We all make mistakes...we need to keep coming back to the Lord for forgiveness and fresh direction!

Quote: "Abraham, after waiting patiently, received what was promised." Hebrews 6:15

11
Why and How should I tell others?

What would have happened if the disciples had kept it to themselves...?

If the Christian faith is really true, then it has to be true for everyone. Everyone should have the chance to hear it shouldn't they?

Fact: The word "GO" appears 1,514 times in the Bible, 223 times in the New Testament and 54 times in Matthew's gospel.

Check out: Matthew 28:16-20

Jesus never said "sit still guys, stay quiet and keep your heads down!"

Jesus told his followers to tell others about him. It's a job that still needs doing today.

> **Fact:** The word "evangelism" means spreading the good news about Jesus.

What worries you about telling your friends?

STRESS POINTS:

* "I don't want to be seen as a religious maniac."

* "I haven't got a clue what to say to people."

* Telling others doesn't mean having to hold a big floppy Bible and stand on street corners shouting at passers-by! It doesn't even mean being an expert in God before you start.

> **Quote:** "I'm being myself in Jesus and he's being himself in me."

So, how do we go about telling people?

1. <u>Just be friendly with people.</u>

" how's life?"

Check out: John 1:40 ...Andrew brought Peter
John 1:45 ...Philip found Nathaniel
John 4:29 ...Woman brought town
Luke 5:29 ...Levi invited friends
Acts 16:34 ...Jailer and his family

And even before thinking about what you will say...

Check out: Matthew 5:13-16

2. Be honest with people.

Sooner or later people will notice something different about you and begin to ask questions.

Simply tell them what's been happening in your life. Tell them what you've experienced.

"So, tell me, Why on earth are you a Christian?"

Fact: A witness gives evidence about something they've seen or experienced.

Check out: Acts 1:8

---

3. <u>Be ready to answer friends questions.</u>

Some friends will have hard questions to ask.
So, think ahead a bit!

Note down some questions people may ask...

Now work out some things you could say to them.

Never be afraid to say, "I don't know the answer to
that question." But try to add, "I could find out for
you though."

See "totally useful" guide at the end of this session.

4. <u>Words are cheap.</u>

* Live it out as well as telling it out.
* Jesus' miracles aroused huge interest.
* Could you offer to pray for someone?

5. <u>Praying.</u>

Pray for your friends.

Pray for yourself to have boldness and to know
what to say and when to say it.

Wrapping it up...!

Don't give up! God will use you as you make yourself available for him.

Check out: Romans 1:16

The Totally Useful **Guide**
Telling your story

a) Don't bore friends - keep your story short.
    3 minutes is about long enough.

b) Don't preach to them-Make
    it personal. It's better to say,
    "I have found that Jesus is great,"
    than, "You must come to Jesus
    right now!" "<u>I</u>" is better than "<u>You</u>"

c) Keep Jesus at the centre of your story.

d) Things to say in your story...

    * a little bit about what you were like before.

    * how you came to know Jesus.

    * something of what your life's been like since.

e) Begin by writing it out on paper - it's easier to
    remember and you can spot the waffle more
    easily!

A prayer that people can pray to help them get to know Jesus.

Lord Jesus,

I'm sorry I haven't got to know you before.
Sorry for the things I've done wrong in my
life. (Take a minute to think of them!)
Please forgive me as I turn from those things.

Thanks for taking the pollution of sin off me
and onto yourself on the cross. Thanks for
forgiving me and setting me free!

Come and make a difference in my life right now.

Come into my life by your Holy Spirit to be with me
forever.

Thank you Lord Jesus. AMEN.

12
Does God heal people today?

Many people have found that he does.
So, what's the evidence?

1. It's in the Bible.

a) Old Testament.

* God made promises about healing. Psalm 41:3

* God is "into" healing. Exodus 15:26

* Examples in the Bible. 2 Kings 5, Isaiah 38,39

b) New Testament and Jesus.

* He taught it.

* He did it!

* He told others to heal

Fact: 25% of the gospels are about healing

- 12 disciples. Matthew 10:1
- 72 of his followers. Luke 10:8-9
- Jesus' last words to his friends. Mark 16:15-20

c) The first Christians.

Check out: Acts 3:1-10 or Acts 5:12-16

2. How to pray for people to get better.

a) In an uncomplicated way.

b) Because we care for them.

Check out: Matthew 9:36, Mark 1:41

"ow, my leg my leg"

c) Using knowledge that God gives.

* Pictures in our minds.

* Having pain in the same place as the person who needs healing.

* Impressions about how we should pray.

* Hearing or seeing words from God.

* Feeling we should say a particular word or
    sentence. It may mean nothing to you, but it
    might mean a lot to the person being prayed for.

d) Pray for them

* Ask them..."where does it hurt?"

* Ask them if they know why they
    have this condition.

* Ask for God's help in directing
    your prayers.

* Ask how are they doing as you
    pray.

* And then care for them in the
    weeks ahead.

"where does it hurt?"

Wrapping it up...!

Keep praying for them...don't give up!

Even doctors don't have a 100% success rate. Yet, they keep being doctors.

If someone is not immediately healed after you've prayed, don't blame anyone or make them feel uncomfortable! Our job is to pray, it's God's job to do the healing!

13
What about the Church?

"Dusty, old, drafty, damp, cold, grey..."

Fact: The church is the people and not the buildings.

The church is not the buildings or the services or the minister or any particular denomination. It's all about people!

1. <u>God's people.</u>

So, if the Church is the people, how do you get in?

Check out: Acts 2:37-41

* Baptism is an outward symbol of what's happening inside a person. Water cleans you outwardly. God cleans up starting on the inside. 1 Corinthians 6:11

* Going under the water then coming up shows that we're part of Jesus' death and resurrection.

* Baptism also helps us remember that God has put his Spirit in our hearts. 1 Corinthians 12:13

a) The Church is BIG!

Check out: Ephesians 3:21

Fact: It's not what you know that makes you part of the church...it's who you know! (ie Jesus)

---

* The Church is more than just a local group. It's worldwide. It even stretches across history.

---

* Presently there are 1,700 million Christians in the world today. They are part of the worldwide Church; people who believe in Jesus.

b) What about local churches?

Check out: Acts 2:42-47

* Like this early church, most churches have a weekly get-together for worship.

* They also have smaller groups as well.

* And sometimes large numbers of Christians have a BIG meeting for worship.

2. Joining the Family.

To show that the Church is all about people, the Bible calls the Church a family.
Galatians 6:10

God is our Father.

If you can imagine what the best Father would be like...

that's what God is like as a
Father and much more!

God wants the Church to stick together too!

Quote: "Make every effort to keep the unity of the Spirit"
Ephesians 4:3

Christians are brothers and sisters to each other.

This means looking out for each other, forgiving when
we upset one another and being together in worship
of God.

3. The Church is called a body.

Check out: Romans 12:4-8

When you run, the bits of your body work together.

They are co-ordinated! The Church is called a body
because God wants us to work together in things.

We may not always like the members of our families, but we still love them. In church people will sometimes annoy us, but we learn to go on loving them.

of course, my organ playing is superior.

4. A living and holy Church.

Check out: Ephesians 2:19-22

So, as the Church we have Jesus holding us together, v.20 and the Holy Spirit living in us. v.22

> **Question:** Where do I fit in...?

Christians should be fully involved with their local church. They should meet with others who believe in Jesus and put into practice what they believe.

Write below the talents God has given you which could be used in the Church.

Talk with your Alpha leader/Youth leader about how you feel as a young person in the Church.

14
Making the most of my life!

Check out: Romans 12:1-21

1. Don't get squeezed.

People have all sorts of ideas
about the way life should be
lived. There may be many voices
crying out "live life this way...
live life that way!"

Quote: "Do not conform any longer to the pattern of this
world." Romans 12:2

Dare to be different. God wants us to live our lives listening to his voice. That doesn't mean being weird! Being a Christian is becoming what God intended us to be in the first place...friendly with him!

Not backbiters...but encouragers.
Not grumblers...but full of joy and life.
Not sleeping around...but keeping God's standards.

What ways will it be difficult for you to be different? (write here)

2. Let God change you.

Let God work in you. He'll show you those areas of your life that need changing for the better.

He'll help you to...Love him and others. v.9

He'll help you to...Be enthusiastic about God. v.11

He'll help you to..Live in peace with others. v.18

3. "Present your bodies"

This is a decision we make. An act of our will.

* ears - listen to good stuff, not gossip or slander.

* eyes - be careful what we watch,especially on TV.

* mouths - don't lie, boast or curse. Use it to praise!

* hands - use them to give and not to take.

* sexuality - God made sex to be enjoyed in marriage.

* time - "Lord, what shall I do for you this week?"

* ambitions. Matthew 6:33

* money - don't be a hoarder, help others by giving.

4. "...as living sacrifices"

* Being a Christian will involve sacrifices.

* It may even involve some suffering.

5. "His good, pleasing and perfect will"

* His plan for your life is:

  - good

  - pleasing

  - perfect

6. "In view of God's mercy..."

* As we look to Jesus, we see how much God loves us.

* And so we cry out to God...Thank you Lord.

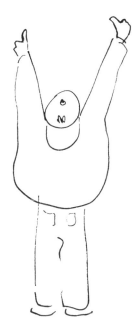